AROUND
HEATHFIELD
IN OLD PHOTOGRAPHS

CROSS IN HAND'S ANNUAL SPORTS DAY on the Hardy Roberts Playing Fields in August 1910. Before a packed grandstand the most entertaining event of the day would have been the animal race featured on the cover. Betting must have been brisk as punters tried to predict the eventual winner from the variety of harnessed animals under starter's orders, including a pig (Lester Piglet, perhaps), chicken, turkey, sheep and a very strange looking monkey. Perhaps the man in the monkey suit is sitting so disconsolately on the fence post because he failed the drug test!

AROUND
HEATHFIELD
IN OLD PHOTOGRAPHS

COLLECTED BY
ALAN GILLET AND
BARRY K. RUSSELL

ALAN SUTTON

Alan Sutton Publishing Limited
Phoenix Mill · Far Thrupp · Stroud · Gloucestershire

First Published 1990
Reprinted 1991

British Library Cataloguing in Publication Data

Around Heathfield in old photographs.
1. East Sussex. Heathfield, history
I. Gillet, Alan *1949–* II. Russell, Barry K. *1946–*
942.251

ISBN 0-86299-714-3

Typeset in 9/10 Korinna.
Typesetting and origination by
Alan Sutton Publishing Limited.
Printed in Great Britain by
The Bath Press, Avon.

CONTENTS

INTRODUCTION

Although Heathfield itself is a 'new' town, the area and its villages can claim a long history. There were Roman roads in this area of the Weald and it was one of the first parts of England to be pacified by the Romans and then by the Normans. It was important enough in medieval times to be granted the right to hold a market and fair in 1315.

Local legend claims Jack Cade, the leader of the peasant rebellion against Henry VI in 1450, as a member of the household of the Dacre family of Bayley Park and, when his army of 40,000 disbanded after promises of clemency from the king, he fled to Newick Farm (now called Cade's Castle). He was hunted down by the newly appointed Sheriff of Kent, Alexander Iden (Cade had killed his predecessor), and mortally wounded by an arrow while playing bowls at Cade Street – probably not named after him but a corruption of Cat Street, as the alehouse the Cat and Shoulder of Mutton stood here. His body was quartered and his head impaled at London Bridge. A commemorative monument was erected at the spot where Iden fired his arrow and a nearby lane still bears Iden's name.

Robert Hunt, vicar of Heathfield from 1602 to 1606, sailed as chaplain with the 1607 expedition to settle the colony of Jamestown, Virginia, the first permanent English colony in North America (thirteen years before the Pilgrim Fathers set sail in the *Mayflower*) and so became the first Christian minister to preach in America.

The most eminent owner of Bayley Park (now known as Heathfield Park) was Lt.-Gen. George Augustus Eliott who bought the estate with prize money he gained at the capture of Havana in 1762. He later successfully defended Gibraltar against combined Spanish and French forces from 1779 to 1783. In recognition of this, he was created Lord Heathfield in 1787. After his death, Gibraltar Tower was erected in the grounds of the park to commemorate his victory.

It may be difficult to believe today, but this very quiet and rural part of the Sussex Weald was Britain's first industrialized area. For nearly two centuries, from the time of Henry VIII onward, iron furnaces and forges produced cannon, shot, firebacks, railings and tools. Iron ore was present locally in the Wadhurst clay; ample supplies of timber from the Wealden forests could be transformed into the charcoal required for the smelting process; and streams like the Cuckmere could be dammed to make the hammer ponds whose water would be used to drive the machinery, the water-powered tilt-hammers of the forges, and the bellows of the furnaces. Tradition maintains that the first iron cannon to be cast in England in one piece (instead of two pieces bonded together) was forged by Ralph Hogge at Hadlow Down in 1543. Indeed, cannon produced in the furnaces of the Heathfield area were highly regarded and were exported to many countries of Europe.

Fortunes were made and several Jacobean manor houses in this area were built by the ironmasters, such as Tanners Manor by the Fullers. Eventually, partly because of the discovery of massive coal deposits elsewhere in the country, the Sussex iron industry dwindled and the last furnace, at Ashburnham, was forced to close in 1825. An unexpected bonus was that vast tracts of woodland had been cleared and these were now available for agricultural cultivation.

The modern histories of both Heathfield and Horam are linked inextricably to the arrival of the railway – indeed even the geographical position of Heathfield was determined by the choice of site of the rail station. The original route selected by the London, Brighton and South Coast Railway involved tunnelling for 1,474 yd beneath Heathfield Park, with the station half a mile from Old Heathfield, just south of the park. However, preliminary investigations revealed potential geological difficulties and the tunnelling route was scrapped. Eventually the route was finalized, with a 266 yd tunnel under Tilsmore Corner with the station (named Heathfield and Cross in Hand) at its southern entrance, one and a half miles away from Old Heathfield (as it is now called) and one mile away from Cross in Hand. The 1875 Ordnance Survey map shows no building of any sort between Tilsmore Corner (with its inn, smithy and nearby windmill) and the lower end of Mutton Hall Hill. By planting Heathfield's station midway between the two villages it was supposed to serve, it opened up this previously undeveloped area for exploitation.

Similarly, when selecting the site of the station to serve Waldron, the LB&SC railway chose a position closer to a neighbouring hamlet: Horeham Road. Even by the turn of the century there were only approximately twenty houses, a newly built church and no shops at all within half a mile of the station. Confusion arose and was compounded by the fact that this new village of Horeham Road sits on the boundaries of three parishes: Hellingly, Heathfield and Waldron, causing administrative chaos – an even more complicated situation than at Heathfield itself where both the High Street and the railway station lay outside Heathfield parish.

The Cuckoo Line, as it was affectionately known, was opened along its southern stretch from Hailsham to Heathfield on 5 April 1880 and then north to Eridge on 1 September 1880, connecting the area directly with London. Five trains a day ran along this single track line, with passing places at each station. The driver would collect a staff entitling him to move on to the next station, where he would deposit the first staff and collect the one for the next section of the route. The line was eventually axed by Dr Beeching with the last train running on 6 May 1968.

The new town of Heathfield gradually developed in the area around the station. By the turn of the century Station Road had been constructed (Neves Bros was the first shop), cutting diagonally from the High Street to The Prince of Wales. The Hailsham Road area was now being developed, including nearby streets like Alexandra Road. In 1899 the first houses and shops were also now appearing along the north side of the High Street. These houses tended to be imposing Victorian middle-class residences, with decorative tiling and woodwork advertising the prosperity of their owner-occupiers. In 1907 the south side of the High Street and much of Station Road had been divided into building plots and community buildings were now being constructed: recreation hall and drill hall (Station Road); agricultural hall (Churwell Road); gas works; and water supply reservoir (mains water was supplied to the High Street area in 1907).

The accidental discovery of natural gas in 1896 while boring for water in the stable-yard of the Station Hotel and, several months later, near the mouth of the rail tunnel produced a flurry of activity in Heathfield over the next few years. A company called the Natural Gas Fields of England Ltd. was formed and began to dig exploratory bore-holes over Heathfield and the surrounding area. Although gas was found, it was only used to light the station (until c. 1930) and nearby streets. (In total seventy to eighty properties were supplied, including the Station Hotel, the major client). Grandiose plans to expand the business by running gas mains to large centres like Brighton and Eastbourne never materialized and the company went into liquidation in 1904.

The chicken-fatting industry was boosted with the arrival of the direct rail link with the London markets. It was Kezia and Joseph Collins, of Keeper's Cottage, Cade Street, who in 1788 realized that money was to be made from buying young fowl from rearers (sometimes through an intermediary, a higgler), force-feeding them to gain weight quickly and delivering the live birds to London where they would fetch higher prices. Other local farmers quickly added the raising and/or fattening of poultry to their business interests and local ironmonger Harry Neve developed a special cramming machine which could be operated by one man. The rail link meant that dead poultry could now be transported – and in much larger quantities. Indeed it is estimated that in the 1890s the Cuckoo Line, and Heathfield Station in particular, was shipping 1,300,000 chickens each year to the London markets where they were sold as Surrey fowl. This trade encouraged other local industries: corn and seed merchants supplied chicken feed ground at the many local wind and watermills; butchers provided tallow (animal fat) and dairies sold milk to bind the cram together; carpenters were required to make coops, crates, peds, etc.; carriers with their carts acted as haulage contractors. It was only the comparatively recent introduction of factory farming which killed off this thriving local business – although Five Ash Down and, until recently, Buxted retained a considerable local link with the poultry industry.

The population of the area has steadily increased during the twentieth century – the most marked expansions being in the two rail towns of Heathfield and Horam. Not even the loss of the railway in 1968 slowed this expansion. Industrial estates are mushrooming, bringing with them new trades and industries, to take the place of others, like brickmaking, which have now died out.

However, many links with the rural past remain: farms, market gardens and nurseries flourish in the area. Gone are the ox-teams, heavy horses and steam traction engines, the working wind- and watermills. Hop gardens may have disappeared and their accompanying oast-houses are probably now converted to desirable residences, but vineyards are becoming increasingly common and quality wine is now produced from local grapes.

This book does not set out to be a complete history of Heathfield and district. It is a book of old photographs and, as such, will only occasionally take the reader beyond the turn of the century. What it does provide, however, is a nostalgic glimpse at the changing scenes and industries of the early decades of this century.

Alan Gillet

SECTION ONE

Heathfield

THE ARRIVAL OF THE RAILWAY brought with it an unexpected and fortuitous discovery. While drilling for a water supply for the steam locomotives in 1896, near the mouth of the tunnel, a strong smell of gas was noticed. A 16 ft flame erupted when a match was applied: natural gas had been found. From 1898 until c. 1930 the station itself utilized the gas from this borehole for lighting; in fact the initial gas pressure was so powerful that normal mantles exploded and fishtail burners had to be used. After 1930 the Ministry of Mines compressed the high grade gas into cylinders for research purposes. The borehole was finally sealed in 1963. Note the gaslamp on the platform and the gasholder on nearby Leeves Common. (c. 1902)

AT TILSMORE CORNER, Ezra Streatfield used to carry on his work as a wheelwright and carriage maker (until c. 1910) in what is now Heathfield Ironmongers. There was a forge to the rear of the adjoining cottages in which Charles Reeve made the iron wheel-rims. A 'To be sold' notice to the extreme right of the illustration shows how the south side of the High Street is only just being developed. (c. 1916)

A CONSIDERABLE TRANSFORMATION HAS NOW TAKEN PLACE. Charlie Ryder built the garage on the junction, close to where the Welcome Stranger had stood. (Eventually Caffyns were to move here from further along the High Street.) He also had The Plaza built, unfortunately with a noisy tin roof, to supersede his showing of silent films at the State Hall. Notice also the gas lamp, the first signs of street lighting. (c. 1925)

ROBERT SOUTHGATE AND HIS WIFE pose outside the furnishing business he set up on Heathfield High Street, specializing in upholstery, cabinet making and sun blinds. The building itself was erected in 1899 and was then extended when first H.B. Dilley and then M.D. and A.E. Preece changed its usage to a bakery, with a bakehouse constructed at the rear. The trees beside the hand cart were only removed in 1972. (c. 1910)

THIS VIEW ALONG THE HIGH STREET shows game hanging outside Edward Moore's fishmonger's shop, which is just receiving a delivery. The next shop along was Fred Deeprose's fruit and vegetable business. Both businesses were set up when the shops were built in 1912. (1912)

FRED NEVE established a millwright's and engineering workshop on the High Street (where Rix & Kay now stands) when he broke the business partnership with his brother in 1912. He was responsible for the repair and maintenance of several of the local windmills.

WORKMEN POSE BESIDE THE TRENCH they have dug along the High Street, outside the original site of Caffyns Garage. Its width and depth suggest it may be the main sewerage system being laid, in the mid-1920s, rather than the main water supply which had been laid along the High Street, Station Road, Marshlands Lane and Tower Street in c. 1907.

A FINE ARRAY OF MOTOR VEHICLES FOR SALE on the forecourt of Caffyns Garage, who were agents for Wolseley, Citroen, Clyno, Swift and Singer cars. Caffyns bought the original three-storey building from Charlie Ryder and soon extended the workshops and showrooms on both sides. (c. 1930)

THE SOUTH SIDE OF THE HIGH STREET was largely dominated by Caffyns Garage. Many of the neighbouring homes and businesses, including the Union Church, had their electrical supply powered by the garage's generator. (c. 1930)

HEATHFIELD HIGH STREET, looking westwards from the original Errey's building, with a man on the roof in the process of painting a large advertisement for the firm. The adjoining shop, with its blind down, was the wine and spirit business of Nelson Kenward. Three girls can be seen escorting a lady in a three-wheeled bath-chair. (1903)

EDWARD ERREY SET UP HIS BUSINESS, dealing initially in second-hand furniture and antiques, in around 1900, with a workshop at the rear to complete repairs. The balcony was used in fine weather to display carpets which could be draped over. In 1910 the business was expanded to include a printing works, hence an asymmetrical third line had to be added to the roof-top advert. This building was destroyed by fire in 1972. (c. 1910)

LOOKING WEST ALONG THE HIGH STREET towards the distant wooded hill at Tilsmore! The original side entrance to Barclays Bank (opened in 1896 and for many years Heathfield's sole bank) has obviously been recently bricked in for a new front entrance to be built. Vera was C.H. Ryder's wife and she ran a ladies' clothing and millinery shop. (c. 1908)

CHARLIE RYDER'S HEATHFIELD STATION GARAGE began life as a bicycle repair shop before he concentrated on motor cycles and motor cars and expanded his business. Notice his claim to fit and repair telephones and bells! The building is now the Red Cross Hall. (1908)

THE ORIGINAL BRITANNIA MILL was completely gutted by fire on 30 April 1907, causing £2,000 worth of damage. Heathfield did not as yet have a fire brigade and there was no telephone to ring Hailsham for help. An eight-mile bicycle ride was necessary before belated assistance arrived. Water was drawn from the nearby mill pond to extinguish the flames, despite the fact that there was already a mains water supply on the High Street.

THE VIEW UP AN UNDEVELOPED MUTTON HALL HILL in 1909, clearly showing John Baitup's recently rebuilt steam-powered corn mill which stood on the corner of Marshlands Lane.

BRITANNIA MILL had been taken over by the London company of Carr, Macdonald and Clevely by the time of this photograph in the mid-1920s. The ground corn and oats were used extensively as poultry food by the many chicken fatteners in the district. Archie Eaton poses next to the vehicle, with Tom Dann under the canopy and Jim Walters to the right.

LOOKING UP MUTTON HALL HILL, with the newly built offices of E. Watson & Son, the auctioneer and estate agent, on the right. By 1910 they required larger premises and built on the corner plot of Station Road, where they remain. The offices were then divided into two shops, and served a variety of business uses until they were demolished. (1910)

LOOKING DOWN MUTTON HALL HILL, clearly showing, on the right, the wooded nature of the area before all the modern developments. The shop on the left, now a ladies' hairdresser, used to be a small dairy. (1903)

SOUTH RIDGE, on which Mutton Hall Hill has grown, viewed from the footpath which ran from the hill to Marshlands Farm, passing alongside Pippins, the white cottage on the far right of the illustration. Housing developments such as Downs View have now blocked this view across to the large house of Southlands (on the left), now flats. Most of the other properties in this photograph are viewed from the rear, and there has been much infilling. Until 1891 a windmill would have been visible on the brow of the hill above Mutton Hall Lane. (1908)

HEATHFIELD TOWER POST OFFICE moved into Samuel Daw's Firlands Stores in c. 1895. (Note the V.R. post box.) The shop also sold groceries, clothes and hardware. It stood on the junction between Mutton Hall Hill and Mutton Hall Lane, directly opposite William Vine's butcher's shop (hence the name Vine's Corner). It is now a private dwelling, retaining the name Firlands. (1909)

TOWER STREET looking from Vine's Corner, during the harsh winter of 1947. The row of cottages on the right were known locally as Donkey Row because of the nickname 'the donkey' given to the alehouse, The Gibraltar Arms, which formed part of the row. (Some of the alehouse's painted advert is still visible today, despite its closing for business in c. 1890.)

TOWER NURSERY stood on the brow of the hill just beyond Vine's Corner. Three generations of William Bean's family pose under the monkey puzzle tree. (c. 1905)

JERVIS'S GARAGE is better known as Crown Garage because of its position close to the Crown Hotel, near the junction with the Battle Road. The business was started by L. Jervis in 1930 and was destroyed by fire during the Second World War. The photograph shows the rebuilt garage in 1952.

THE CROWN HOTEL HEATHFIELD.

THE CROWN HOTEL moved to its present site early in the nineteenth century and for many years served as the local corn exchange. Behind the buildings, which include Ebenezer Evenden's printing workshop, is the market site. Heathfield was granted permission to hold a market by the lord of the manor, the Bishop of Chichester, in 1315.

BERT ELDRIDGE'S GROCERY STORE (now an Indian restaurant) stood next to the market site. It was built on the site of John Valentine's grocery shop which, until c. 1895 served as post office for Heathfield Common, the name given originally to the area around Vine's Corner and The Crown. The mail coach between Hawkhurst and Lewes used to drop the local mail off here. (1935)

LOOKING NORTH ALONG HAILSHAM ROAD. Beyond the parade of shops, apparently sideways on to the road, stands The Prince of Wales which is first mentioned as a licensed premises in 1867. Although it now stands prominently on a road junction, it was operating as an ale-house long before Station Road was built alongside it. (1903)

LOOKING SOUTH ALONG HAILSHAM ROAD from The Prince of Wales. Amazingly the shop on the corner of Upper Station Road seems to have been an off-licence since its erection at the turn of the century. In this 1915 postcard view it is a tied off-licence of local brewer Ballard & Co., being managed by William Butcher, who also incorporated a grocery business.

THE DRAPER'S AND MILLINER'S SHOP on Hailsham Road, with Vale View Road on the right, was run by Mrs Nellie Francis and her family. She also ran a second shop at Horeham Road. The strange framework jutting up from the edge of the pavement was used to fasten the sunblind to, as with the adjoining shop, which from the turn of the century has been Hailsham Road's post office. For many years Mrs Josephine Farley was sub-postmistress here. (1909)

COLLINGWOOD RISE was constructed by local builder Frank Collins in c. 1930 on the site of what had earlier been William Knight's Park Nurseries, hence its original name Park Nurseries Estate.

SANDY CROSS STORES, here run by Edward Funnell, stood on the Ghyll Road junction, only very recently blocked to traffic. For many years the shop was to be run by Richard and later Mrs Relf. Today it concentrates on selling washing machines. (c. 1910)

AN EARLY HACKNEY CARRIAGE outside Sandy Cross Stores. Although the chassis and engine would be supplied from the motor manufacturer, the bodywork of such a taxi would have been built to individual specifications by a local coach works. Somehow I don't think its bald tyres (and spare) would pass the present MOT tests.

SANDY CROSS POSTMILL stood just south-east of the junction, alongside the main road, and was operated by Walter and George Knight until its demolition in 1916. Charles Haffenden can be seen carrying a bucket of water back from the well at the mill. The building on the left is Sandy Cross Stores. (1910)

SANDY CROSS LANE sloping down towards the thatched Monkhurst farmhouse. In around 1930 a flat tin roof replaced the oast-house's distinctive roof and cowl and the oast was used to house pigs. Today a tasteful renovation and conversion to a private dwelling is underway. Much damage was caused to houses in the area, and some injuries, when a doodle-bug was shot down by fighters on 29 June 1944. (c. 1910)

THE WATER MAINS being laid along Hailsham Road. The labourers must have been tough in those days, handling the sections of iron pipe (only flanged at one end) with bare hands in those icy conditions. The clothing of the lady and little boy in the distance suggest a day of perhaps 1910. The magnificent example of topiary stood outside Yew Tree Cottage, near Sandy Cross.

OVER THE RIDGE OF PROSPECT ROAD from what used to be called locally Bubbs Hill, there were magnificent easterly views over Heathfield Park. Now, alas, the view is likely to be of the 400 rooftops of the new Green Lane estate. Dalhousie, built in 1878 as a single dwelling, has since been divided. (c. 1910)

ALEXANDRA ROAD IN THE SNOW, c. 1910. The church is set back behind the trees on the left, while Brightling House and Dorrie Lodge were only built in 1911.

CLOSE TO THE WELCOME MISSION HALL, built in 1886 by local subscription and originally called the Gilbert Hall, the Neve brothers constructed an unusual sixteen-bladed wind-wheel to provide the power for George Rumary's carpentry workshop on Alexandra Road. The workshop only ceased operating in the mid-1970s although the wind-wheel, a smock-mill structure built on part of its roof, had long been demolished. (c. 1910)

THE VIEW UP STATION ROAD, with a number of items on display outside Neve Bros' shop, including two chicken crammers. The eastern side of Station Road remains undeveloped at the time of this photograph in 1906.

NEVE BROTHERS (HARRY AND FRED) started trading in Station Road in 1895. (They had originally worked as millwrights with their father Stephen Neve at Flitterbrook Lane, Punnetts Town.) As well as the ironmonger's shop, there was an adjoining workshop and forge. It was presumably here that Harry Neve invented his chicken crammer. The Neve family connection with the shop only ceased in 1970. (c. 1895)

BOMB DAMAGE TO NEVE'S SHOP on Station Road, probably from the bomb explosion to the south-west of Marshlands Lane which smashed many windows along the High Street and Station Road. Helping to clear the display window of the glass fragments is Grace Neve.

THIS POSTCARD OF STATION ROAD in 1913 reveals the extent to which this area was developed in those intervening few years, presenting a view which is still easily recognizable today, with shops, offices and the recreation hall all recently built. The fencing alongside 'Monkey' Durrant's cart marks the intended route of a new road which was never constructed.

A SUPERB STUDY OF A CHICKEN CRAMMER AT WORK. The machine, invented by Harry Neve, was an improvement on earlier designs because it was easily manoeuvrable and could be operated by one man, who could work the treadle with his foot and hold the bird with his two hands. The cram was mixed into a paste – traditionally a combination of oats, tallow (rendered down animal fat) and milk (when available, blown tins of evaporated milk were substituted) – and poured into the hopper. One press with the foot would plunge a measured quantity of the cram directly into the crop of the bird, along the eight inches of india rubber tubing which had been forced down its throat. In this way chicks could quadruple their weight in several weeks. On either side can be seen the raised fattening coops (holding up to fifteen birds each) which would be covered by sacking at night.

AFTER KILLING, the chickens would be plucked and the feathers allowed to fall into bodges, rough wooden troughs at the pluckers' feet. Women traditionally did the stubbing, pinching out the new feathers and any remaining stubs. Usually the bird was then turned quickly over a flame to singe what still remained (called sweeling). Finally the birds would be powdered with flour and placed in a press, with their breasts downwards, to give the bird the appearance of having a plumper breast.

PACKING FOR MARKET. After a period in the press, the birds would be carefully packed into peds, specially built wooden crates which could transport up to two dozen chickens, with straw between each layer. The full peds would then be taken to Heathfield station by carrier, for shipment to one of the London markets, and then returned to the farmer for future use.

F.W. HOGBEN'S GROCERY STORE was built at Station Road in 1913, where Wildblood's now stands, and Bert Eldridge was the manager. He was to transfer his business to the High Street during the Second World War. What impressive pyramids of tins and packages fill the display windows, with many of the items still available today: Scotts Porage [*sic*] Oats and Shippams Potted Meats! (*c.* 1930)

THE RECREATION (OR STATE) HALL was built in 1909 to serve as a local centre for all types of entertainment: concerts, dances, parties – even roller skating and (silent) cinema shows. From 1962 (until 1990) it became a garment workshop of P. Moss, making kilts, etc. The frontage of this large building used to contain two shops: on the left stood Fred Stevens' jewellery shop (he was also chairman of Heathfield United Football Club) and on the left Edward Crisp's chemist shop. (1930)

A MEET OF FOXHOUNDS outside Station Hotel. It was built C. 1895 on the site of farm buildings which had belonged to the Heathfield Park Estate and was finally demolished in 1984. Apparently hunts were eventually discouraged in the Heathfield area with the increase of poultry farming throughout the locality. (1908)

THE OFFICES AND SHOP OF BUILDER, FRANK COLLINS, on the junction of Station Road and Station Approach (now Coffee Break). Some of the decorative scrollwork of the original window frames can still be seen. His builder's yard was further along Station Road on the site of what had been Park Nurseries.

LOOKING OVER THE ROAD BRIDGE across the railway lines with the railway station on the right and the original Temperance Hotel on the left. In the distance can be seen the Station Hotel, with a heavily laden cart in front. The roof of the recreation hall is clearly visible. (c. 1920)

WALDRON THORNS ESTATE was built in 1949, linking Station Approach with Ghyll Road. It is difficult to believe that there was ever a time when the road was free of double parked cars.

THE ORIGINAL TEMPERANCE HOTEL was built in 1900 on the eastern side of the rail bridge, for George Winter. It was a family hotel in which no alcohol would be served. As well as comfortable accommodation, there was a dining room and small grocery shop at the front. For many years it was run by Mrs Mary Avard, who eventually sold the building to the Lewes (later Brighton) Co-operative Society. (c. 1920)

THE NEW TEMPERANCE HOTEL, slightly smaller than the original, was built in 1924 on the west side of the rail bridge for Mrs Mary Avard, who again ran a tea rooms at the front which served as the railway station buffet. To the left of the building her son Bill operated a taxi service. Heathfield's first petrol pump stood here.

HEATHFIELD STATION, viewed from the Twitten, above the 266 yd tunnel. In the foreground is the water tank and, just visible directly behind, are the two gas holders, containing natural gas used for lighting the station and pumping the water. Beyond the road bridge is the fully glazed passenger footbridge. (1930)

THE TRAIN FOR HAILSHAM stands steaming at the station in this view of the main line and the goods sidings, taken from Strickland's Grain Stores. The station itself is masked by the smoke, but directly above can be seen the railworkers' cottages on the Twitten. The goods shed stands in the centre of the shot. (1910)

THE GOODS YARD where George Giles, who was for many years landlord of The Prince of Wales and also grew hops where Nursery Way now stands, receives a delivery of coal, each sack being measured out on the large scoop scales in the centre. Behind is the roof of the goods shed and, to the right, the station master's house. On the horizon can be seen the windmill which (until c. 1890) stood on Mill Road, then known as Carter's Lane, and, to its right, Tilsmore (now Holdenhurst).

TRAIN DERAILMENT AT TOOTH'S BANK, two and a half miles north of Heathfield, at 9 a.m. on 1 September 1897. The class D1 engine *Bonchurch* was running north on this hilly and curved stretch of line when it derailed and toppled over. The engine itself remained on top of the embankment but the carriages slid down the slope, crushing the train driver, James McKenly, who had been thrown clear. (He was the only fatality.)

THE EXISTENCE OF THE RAILWAY spawned a variety of local businesses, among them the carriers, who could collect and deliver items all over the neighbourhood. The 'Heathfield Transport Co. Ltd' ran their coal, corn and animal food business from this corrugated building in the railway station yard and were official agents for Southern Railway. (c. 1925)

DELIVERY CART OF WILLIAM COLLINS. He used to run his coal business from Alexandra Road until the beginning of the First World War when he moved to new premises on Station Road (where Hugh Page Ltd now stands) and expanded his business to include furniture removal and 'Motor, Steam & Horse Haulage'.

LOOKING DOWN STATION ROAD, with Strickland's Grain Warehouse, now Apex Mill, on the left and, further along, the goods yards of the railway station. By 1920 Strickland's were using an engine-driven machine to mill their own corn on the premises. (c. 1904)

UPPER STATION ROAD was only developed by local builder George Rumary in c. 1910. John Catt set up his grocery business (later more of a general store) in 1911. It was later run by Annie Catt and her daughter. There was an old bakery behind the premises. The first house became the local police station when Sergeant Hill lived there while Church End was owned by St Richard's church and for many years housed its curate. (c. 1920)

NATURAL GAS FIELDS OF ENGLAND LTD was the name of the company formed in 1902 to drill for gas in the Heathfield area. Six holes were drilled in Heathfield itself, all within three-quarters of a mile of the station, with several others in the surrounding area: two at Mayfield and one each at Netherfield, Ticehurst, Crowborough and Wadhurst. By November 1904 the company was forced to go into liquidation. (c. 1902)

STEAM RISES from the steam-powered machinery working on the site of No. 3 Boring on the banks of the wooded valley of Waldron Gill. The houses in the distance are Marshlands Farm and Lyndhurst on Marshlands Lane, while the silhouette of the Gibraltar Tower is masked by trees on the skyline. This same view today would encompass several hundred houses! (1902)

A CYLINDRICAL GAS HOLDER is constructed on the wasteland off Station Road – directly behind the original Temperance Hotel – with the Station Hotel in the background. A similar gas holder was constructed on Marshlands Lane – hence its local nickname of Gasworks Lane – but this was used for storing normal town gas. (c. 1902)

RELEASE OF BALLOONS FILLED WITH NATURAL GAS from Heathfield railway station on Edward VII's coronation day, 9 August 1902. It also served as part of a publicity campaign to advertise the discovery of natural gas and the setting up of the company to exploit it, the Natural Gas Fields of England Ltd. One balloon travelled 600 miles within 24 hours and it was picked up the following day at Ulm in southern Germany. On the right is the covered footbridge, while on the skyline are the railworkers' cottages on the Twitten, directly above the rail tunnel.

LOOKING ALONG TILSMORE ROAD from Tilsmore Corner, with Salcombe Lodge and Lee House on the left, the distinctive chimney having now disappeared. (1930)

WALDRON THORNS is correctly the name of the open area of land which used to lie to the north of Geer's Wood, bisected by Ghyll Road. The illustration shows a sharp bend in the charmingly named Pook Reed Lane, with the footpath over the style leading to Ghyll Road. The roof of The Dene can be seen to the right. (1909)

LOOKING UP GHYLL ROAD from Stream Bridge, which crosses Waldron Gill at the foot of the valley. Geer's Wood, the considerable area of woodland to the left of this illustration, has recently been transformed into a large housing development.

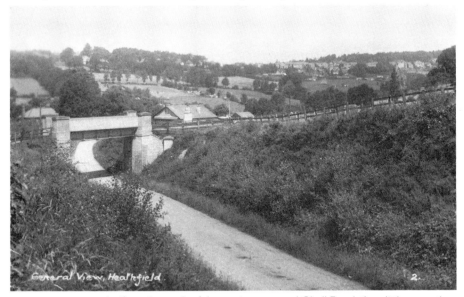

THE RAILWAY BRIDGE, half a mile south of the station, crossed Ghyll Road, then little more than a country lane in appearance, near French's Farm at Sandy Cross. Little of this rural tranquillity remains, with housing developments and industrial estates replacing the charm of the railway line. (1930)

HEATHFIELD PARK CRICKET CLUB was founded in 1878, with its grounds within the Park; surely one of the most beautiful cricket grounds in the county. Behind the team can be seen the original pavilion, replaced first in 1936 and again in 1973.

HEATHFIELD UNITED FOOTBALL CLUB in the 1907/8 season. At this time the club played its home matches on a pitch to the south of Sheepsetting Lane.

HEATHFIELD LADIES' STOOLBALL TEAM in 1912, a game played exclusively in Sussex and Kent. Seated alongside the stoolball bats and holding the scorebook is Eric Bean who appears in several of the other Heathfield photographs.

HEATHFIELD HOCKEY TEAM plays a mixed match on Tower Street Recreation Ground. The club was disbanded in the late 1950s. In the background can be seen Page's Hill school, a private school, set back from Mutton Hall Hill, now Page's Cottages. (c. 1950)

HEATHFIELD GYM CLUB strike up a variety of balancing poses to impress the cameraman.

HEATHFIELD'S FIRST BAND was a fife and drum band formed in c. 1888, sometimes nicknamed the Chicken Fatters Band. For a number of years it developed into a military brass band, and became a detachment of the Second Sussex Royal Garrison Artillery Volunteers' Brass Band for forty years. (1922)

HEATHFIELD TOBACCO FUND was one of several fund-raising activities designed to alleviate the lot of the troops serving during the First World War. The money raised by local soldier, Private Luther Leeves, while on leave, would be used to purchase tobacco to be sent out to the trenches. The caption on this 1916 postcard, 'Let Brotherly Love Continue', is hardly appropriate!

THE SILVER QUEEN AIRSHIP of the RNAS flies gracefully over the roof of the Station Hotel. The small gondola underneath the non-rigid airship was the fuselage of a small monoplane (an Armstrong Whitworth FK3) and was only large enough to carry the pilot. During the First World War she was stationed near Wannock and was used extensively along the Channel coast for submarine detection. (c. 1916)

AN ALBION CHARABANC collects the ladies of the Heathfield Sisterhood for their annual outing in 1924. They used to meet in the Agricultural Hall in Cherwell Road (built in c. 1900 as the Natural Gas Showroom but now Errey's storeroom) until joining with the Brotherhood in the early 1930s. Behind can be seen the clothing stores of Long, Fry & Howes.

NELSON KENWARD'S WINE SHOP on the High Street had to rely on a horse and cart for its deliveries until a motor van was purchased in 1913. Ben Burgess poses alongside one of the later delivery vans.

HEATHFIELD'S AIR RAID WARDENS, Len Strange, Ray Collins, Frank Neve and Tommy Saunders, check their supply of gas masks and filters at Collingwood Rise during the Second World War.

BOMB DAMAGE IN THE GARDEN of Hillcrest, Collingwood Rise – ironically within fifty yards of the above photograph – in September 1940. Mrs Stokes and ARP Warden Tommy Saunders inspect the crater. Amazingly there was no structural damage to the house itself.

HEATHFIELD AND WALDRON FIRE BRIGADE was inaugurated as a joint venture between the two parish councils in 1924. The original engine, a converted Model T Ford affectionately nicknamed Auntie, was purchased in 1925. A garage was built alongside the bus depot (now Southern Boat Co.) on Tilsmore Road in 1926, with Charlie Ryder (local garage and cinema owner) as the chief officer. Initially the crew was called out by maroons. (1926)

'GET ME TO THE CHURCH ON TIME'. What better than for Eric (better known as Pete) and Ella Bean to borrow Heathfield's newly converted Model A Ford fire engine for their wedding transport at All Saints' church, Old Heathfield, in 1932. Note the hand bell (no flashing lights or sirens yet) and the fire extinguisher.

Old Heathfield

Cuckoo Fair, Heathfield.

T. Sharp, Heathfield, Sussex.

THE CUCKOO FAIR was one of two annual stock fairs granted to Heathfield in 1315. The spring fair was called the Cuckoo Fair because the first cuckoo in England was traditionally released from a basket by an old woman at the fair. It was held on 14 April in the fields – and roads – around the Half Moon Inn. Gypsy caravans, selling anything from horses to clothes pegs, would park all along the road to the church. (c. 1908)

THE OLD HALF MOON INN used to stand on the Hawkhurst Road opposite the Newick Lane junction, but it closed when the road was re-routed to follow the crest of the ridge rather than hugging the park wall. The new Half Moon was rebuilt at Cade Street, but changed its name to the Jack Cade about ten years ago. Alfred Allchin's baker's handcart stands outside the bakery on the corner, with W. Brown's horse-drawn cart in front of the drill hall. (They were an important carrier at the station and also ran a coal and corn business.) (c. 1910)

HARMER HOUSE, built in 1661 of Portland stone (hence the name Portland Square), served as the village bakehouse in the eighteenth century and it was probably in the same ovens that Jonathan Harmer dried out his terracotta bas-reliefs c. 1800–c. 1840. Another occupant, Michael Harmer, took three years to build the three miles of stone wall around the park (c. 1836), some of which is visible to the right. In 1909 Thomas Evenden ran a newsagent's shop at the house.

THE ANCIENT ORDER OF FORESTERS pose with their families outside Cade Street's drill hall, alongside the Half Moon. The Drill Hall was where the local men enlisted for military service during the wars. (C. 1932)

THE LOCAL SQUADRON OF AIR TRAINING CORPS CADETS stand to attention at Cade Street during Battle of Britain year, 1940. Behind can be seen the single-storeyed building which was for many years Henry Ticehurst's butcher's shop. The building to the left, until very recently the post office, used to serve as the local confectioner's.

BARROW'S GENERAL STORE (C. 1910) used to be the original Crown Inn. Thomas Barrow opened the shop here in 1840, later helped by his four sons, and it was soon adopted as Heathfield Post Office and later extended. In 1944 it suffered damage from a flying bomb which exploded nearby. The shop was closed around 1975.

TWISSELL'S MILL, the beautiful half-timbered watermill to the south of Heathfield Park, operated until October 1909 when sluice gates at the Park's four lakes were opened, causing the mill pond to overflow and the mill cottage, where the miller Tim Oliver lived, to be flooded.

EASTBOURNE HUNT meet at Heathfield Park c. 1905. The house itself was built in around 1500 by Lord Dacre. In 1766 Lt.-Gen. George Eliott, the heroic defender of Gibraltar, later named Lord Heathfield, bought the estate with prize money gained from the capture of Havana in 1762. In recent years an unsuccessful attempt was made to transform the estate into a wildlife park.

A LOCAL SCOUT TROOP with their pipes, drums, triangle and flags pose proudly on the steps of Heathfield Park.

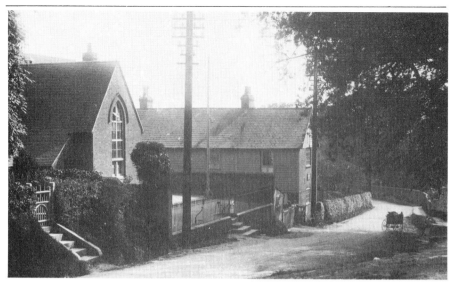

HEATHFIELD NATIONAL SCHOOL, now a church-aided primary school, was built in 1819 from parish subscriptions. It was called the round school because of its original shape, with its one large circular room and a central fire. It was rebuilt much closer to the church along more traditional lines. The building alongside, Quince Tree Cottage, served as the premises for John Payne, builder and undertaker.

HOP FIELDS flourished throughout the area; the number of oast-houses attest to this. Men would cut down the bines and uproot the poles, allowing the women – and often their children – to pick the hops into the bins (hessian bags supported on wooden frames). The hops would be measured in wicker baskets and transported to the oast-house for drying. The scene shows hop picking probably on the site of the old Furnace Pond, at Pond Farm. Although there is now no trace of the furnace itself, slag and clinker can be found in the blackened soil. (1911)

SCHOOL HILL leads past Beech Cottage (on the left) which used to house the local schoolmistress until 1850 and has also been a dairy. Facing is Home Cottage, originally two cottages. Still visible, on its side wall, are three stone faces, representing the builder and his sons, and a terracotta cooper, hence the current name for the property, Cooper's Spinney. (c. 1910)

THE OLD COTTAGES which lead to the Star formed part of the ancient village of Heathfield which grew up around the church, but they are now almost hidden from view behind high hedges. The carpentry workshop on the corner has long been demolished. Directly opposite, at the entrance to Heathfield House, stood the parish workhouse. (1910)

THIS 1910 VIEW OF ALL SAINTS' CHURCH reveals many changes. The church tower only had its clock added in 1920; the three Priors Cottages on the left were demolished in c. 1915; while the Star Inn had the stables demolished in the mid-1960s in order to extend its car park. Inside All Saints' church can be found an inscription, G.S. 1445, apparently the oldest authenticated date in arabic numerals in England.

THE STAR INN was built in the fourteenth century to act as a hostelry for the army of stonemasons required to rebuild the church after a disastrous fire in 1380 – and has continued to serve the community ever since. The corner of the building, now Star Inn Cottage, used to be a butcher's shop.

Broad Oak

ISAAC MOCKFORD poses outside his general store built opposite the broad oak which was to give this area its name. He seems to have sold almost everything, including his own postcards and guidebooks. For many years the shop served as the local post office and, indeed, the sorting office for the whole of the Heathfield area. The building itself had to be expanded outwards and upwards but was finally demolished to allow the road to be widened. (c. 1890)

BROAD OAK MILL – a post-mill – stood on the ridge to the north of the main road, close to where the electricity sub-station now stands. It was destroyed by fire on 11 March 1890 and there are no visible remains to be seen today.

THE NEWSAGENT'S SHOP AT BROAD OAK, with a fine display of adverts: cigarettes at ten for 4d. (1½p); a glass of sparkling drink for 1d.; and the *Daily Telegraph* for 1d. The news article by Mr Baldwin and the 'Remembrance' issue suggest a date of 1936, when George V died and Stanley Baldwin was prime minister. The delivery van is a Morris.

LOOKING EAST TOWARDS THE CROSSROADS c. 1910. At this time there was very little development on the south side of the main road. In the distance can be seen the oast-house alongside which stood the old ale-house, the Spotted Cow (now a private dwelling).

THE CROSSROADS AT BROAD OAK showing the two-storeyed general store of Isaac Mockford on the right. On the opposite junction stood William Malpass's smithy. (He had another at Quarry Brook.) The smithy had to be demolished and rebuilt further over to the left when Halley Road was widened. (c. 1904)

EBENEZER STRICT BAPTIST CHAPEL was built in 1859 by George Mockford, with the local cemetery adjoining. The advertisement on the right is for E. Richardson's Corn Stores. (c. 1904)

BROAD OAK SCHOOL was built on Scotsford Road in 1911 to cater for 160 children, with the school house alongside which now serves as the office, etc. The strange projection above the windows of the old school hall is for the school bell.

A HOME-MADE CRATE-SCYTHE being used at Little Binns Farm, Swife Lane, by Charlie Pankhurst. The outer frame was intended to push the hay and grass forward as it was being cut (unlike the normal scythe), almost forming stooks as it falls. (c. 1940)

A FARMAN BIPLANE, flown by a French pilot, Barras, was forced to land in a hay field near Rock Hill, between Broad Oak and Burwash Common, to get mechanical repairs before continuing in the air race from Dover to Hendon on 3 July 1911. School groups from miles around – and interested adults – came to view this early aeroplane.

ROCKHILL MILL stood on high ground to the left of the main road between Broad Oak and Burwash Common. It was a post-mill with a single-storeyed roundhouse and was operated by the Dallaway family. It ceased working during the First World War and, by the time of this 1935 photograph, was already in a sorry condition, having lost its sweeps, and some strips from its metalled sides. (1935)

Punnett's Town and Three Cups

BLACKDOWN MILL, also known as Cherry Clack Mill, originally stood at Biddenden, Kent, and was dismantled and brought to its current position in 1859 to replace the post-mill which was burnt to the ground in that same year. This 1875 photograph of the smock-mill shows Samuel Dallaway, the miller, in the granary doorway; his son Thomas on the stage; and son Charles at the head of the cart. It is the sole survivor of the three Punnett's Town mills.

SCHOOL ROAD, looking east, with the school to the left of the posed pupils, with the recreation ground opposite. The mound of flint chippings at the junction would be used for infilling and road repairs. Originally no steam rollers were used; the stones would be bedded in naturally, from the constant use of passing cartwheels, etc. (1910)

PUNNETT'S TOWN SCHOOL was built in 1879 as a mixed elementary school, originally with two classrooms, but a third was added later. Its total capacity was 150 children. Like many schools in this area, it offered a wartime haven for evacuees from London during the early period of the Second World War. (c. 1910)

PUNNETT'S TOWN'S WARTIME FIRE SERVICE. In 1939 Punnett's Town had a stirrup pump to combat fires and had to use the old wooden cricket pavilion as its headquarters. Its new fire station became a sports pavilion and later the village hall after the war. Volunteers could opt for the national fire service instead of the home guard. In the picture are: E. Wood, S. Harvey, E. Oliver, T. Frogbrook, B. Thompson, W. Pettit, R. Walters, F. Ellis, S. Wood. E. Parsons, T. Ellis, W. Burchett, H. Burchett, T. Salter, G. Ditch.

PUNNETT'S TOWN'S VICTORY TREAT, to celebrate the end of the war in Europe, was held in September 1945. It is noticeable that the group consists mainly of women and children as most of the able-bodied men of the village would still be on active service. At the back, with the school behind them, stand the uniformed men of the local National Fire Service.

THE FREAK WEATHER CONDITIONS of March 1947, when snow thawed and then immediately refroze, caused damage throughout the neighbourhood. Here, looking from Huglett's Lane towards Chapel Cross, all the telegraph lines have snapped under the weight of the icicles.

THE FINGER POST at Chapel Cross (not strictly a cross road but a T-Junction) marks the junction of the B2096 (Battle to Heathfield road) with the country road leading to Warbleton, near the site of the Independent Chapel. Horse drawn carts were still a common sight on the roads in the 1930s.

UNVEILING of the Heathfield and Warbleton Protestant Martyrs' Memorial by General Sir William Stirling KCB on 27 September 1905, outside the Independent Chapel, before a crowd of 2,000 people. This obelisk commemorated the martyrdom of ten Sussex Protestants who were burnt to death at Lewes in 1557 during the religious persecution of Mary Tudor's reign (including Richard Woodman and George Stevens of Warbleton and Margery Morris and her son James of Cade Street).

ROBERT STURDY (second from left) and his fleet of vehicles, including a model T Ford, an ex-army ambulance and two Hallford's lorries with solid wheels. His business was as a haulage contractor and coal merchant. (1920s)

PUNNETT'S TOWN'S SECOND SMOCK-MILL, octagonal in shape, drove the three circular saws of Lower & Piper's workshop, a timber structure positioned directly underneath. It was transferred from Horam in 1866 and continued to operate until wind-power was replaced by an engine in 1927. This rare wind-powered saw-mill was demolished in 1933. (c. 1910)

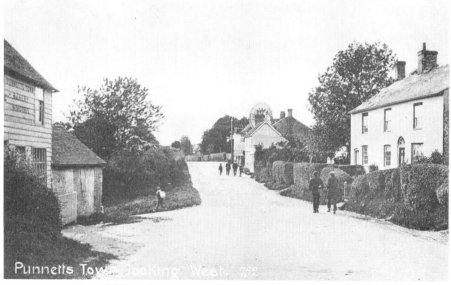

LOOKING WEST from William Morris's bakery, we can see the seventy-vaned wind-wheel which supplied the power for Sampson Punnett's carpentry workshop. Built by the Neves on the site of what became Cornford's grocery stores, it was dismantled approximately ten years later in 1916. (1908)

THE BARLEY MOW with Pont's Stores alongside. The frontage and roofline of the pub have been considerably reconstructed. Opposite stands Luck's Farm, for many years the home of the Punnett family, after whom the village is named. (c. 1908)

PONT'S STORES, run until 1895 by Mr Burgess, stood next to the Barley Mow and was seen as the hub of the village, selling everything from groceries, sweets, patent medicines, china, hardware and even drapery. It became the village post office – originally at James Buckman's shop – and retained its link with the Pont family until the death of Percy Pont (centre) in 1949.

NORTH STREET, opposite William Morris's bakery, was the site of Punnett's Town's post office prior to its move to Pont's. James Buckman was the sub-postmaster, grocer and draper, but it has already ceased trading and is boarded up in this postcard. There were apparently two other bakers at this bottom end of North Street and Joseph Oliver ran a smithy and wheelwright's workshop at the top end where Gretna now stands. (c. 1925)

PUNNETT'S TOWN FOOTBALL TEAM, nicknamed The City (hence the badge's initials: CFC), pose with some of their trophies c. 1918.

THE THREE CUPS INN C. 1910, long before the front porches were added. Notice the magnificent oil lantern behind the landlord James Trill's head, with its reflector clearly visible. Using half-barrels as plant tubs is obviously not such a new idea after all!

THREE CUPS CORNER, looking along the main road from Battle to Heathfield, across the open ground which serves as the forecourt of the Three Cups Inn, with Eastwood's General Store on the left (now a dairy). The chapel at Three Cups has recently been converted into a religious centre.

A STANDARD FORDSON TRACTOR, driven by Sid Hook, pulls a binder on Coppice Farm, Turner's Green. Note its iron-spiked wheel, its crank-handle and its power take-off pulley which could drive saw benches, chaff cutters and other machinery. (1920s)

MESSAGE'S BRICKYARD, at Turner's Green, was one of three such brickyards in the immediate area. Each workman was allocated a hut in which he would work the locally dug loam to the correct consistency before putting it into the moulds. These 'green' bricks were then stacked in a long shed (off camera to the left) for drying prior to firing in the kilns. In the centre can be seen the horse-drawn pug-wheel used for mixing the finely textured clay necessary for tile-making. (1920s)

SECTION FIVE

Warbleton and Rushlake Green

PED MAKING at Turner's Green (c. 1935). Edward Lulham uses a draw-knife to complete the basic framework of a 'ped', a re-usable crate for transporting dead chickens (usually by train to London).

A BEAUTIFUL ANIMATED STUDY of visitors to The Horse and Groom in c. 1850, when the landlord was Trayton Burgess. The costumes are magnificent, from the smocks and working clothes of the rustics to the hooped skirts of the ladies and waistcoats of the gentlemen.

WARBLETON FRIENDLY SOCIETY, really a local 'insurance' scheme which covered the members for sickness and funeral expenses, was founded in 1855. Any profit was used to subsidize the annual feast day in May when members, wearing their blue and red rosettes, would meet at Rushlake Green, march to the parish church accompanied by a band, then march back to the Horse and Groom for a meal of roast beef followed by Christmas pudding! (1888)

CRICKET WAS FIRST PLAYED ON THE GREEN in 1747, according to local tradition, and continued to be played there until 1946. Because of the size and shape of the green, local rules had to be adopted, namely: boundaries to the edge of the green – three runs; shots which cleared the green – four runs; shots which cleared neighbouring buildings – six runs. (c. 1905)

A GROUP OF SPECTATORS, including the local postman, admire the performance of the local cricket team in about 1910, while the scorers sit at the entrance to their tent. The building on the left is the village school.

THE GENERAL STORES OF BOOKER AND OSBORNE with their horse-drawn delivery wagon posed outside. It is tempting to suggest that the man in the goggles in the rather exotic looking car, possibly a de Dion, might be Dr Burfield, who owned the first motor vehicle in the village. (c. 1910)

WILLIAM OXLEY'S BAKERY and grocer's shop – now a private residence – at the north-east of the green, as it appeared 100 years ago. Presumably a delivery is expected, since the trap doors to the cellar are open. It had earlier been converted from a mission hall. (c. 1890)

A VIEW ACROSS THE GREEN showing Booker and Osborne's general store (far left) and the bakery, now being run by William Dumbrell, directly behind the horse and cart.

Rushlake Green, Warbleton, 455.

THE SHOP WHICH IS NOW THE POST OFFICE stands to the south of the green. It was opened in c. 1885 as a grocer's shop for Albert Atkinson, but for most of the twentieth century it has been owned and run by the Daw family. In the distance can be seen the inn sign for The Horse and Groom. (1906)

A DIAGONAL VIEW ACROSS THE TRIANGULAR GREEN in the centre of the village. The three children posing in the centre give it an impression of increased size. Fern Villa was built in the nineteenth century for the village policeman. On the right can be seen the school, with its delightful bell tower. (c. 1918)

THE VILLAGE ELEMENTARY SCHOOL was built in 1873 to accommodate up to 160 children. It was built on a rather grand scale typical of the Victorian Gothic style, replacing the original school which had operated on the opposite side of the green since 1812. In 1965 it closed down and is now an old people's home, Osborne House.

THE OLD WOODEN SCOUT HALL to the south of the village green was demolished to make way for the Dunn Village Hall, built on its site.

TRAVELLING FAIRS such as Pettigrew's would sometimes set up their roundabouts and stalls on the green to add to the local entertainment of the feast day. This often caused aggravation to the village cricket club, however, who would then have to cope with the tracks left by traction engines on their outfield. (1910)

SUMMERHILL MILL, a white weather-boarded post-mill to the north of Chapman's Town, was built in 1824 and stopped working in 1914. When this photograph was taken in 1935, the mill owners, Ellis Bros, had already stripped out all the internal machinery for the power-driven mill which was operated alongside. In 1936 the derelict mill was pulled down by a traction engine, leaving the round-house intact for storage purposes, etc.

THE HORSE-DRAWN DELIVERY WAGON of Ellis Bros' Summerhill Mill, supervised by Messrs Ellis and Foster, has stopped for the horse's lunch at Three Cups.

GEORGE HOOK TRANSFERS MILK left for collection at the dairy of a Three Cups farm into his own churns, prior to its delivery to a dairy at Heathfield. The boxes on top of the seventeen-gallon milk churns were presumably for transporting eggs. Note the wooden-spoked wheels with solid tyres.

A YOKED TEAM OF OXEN, driven by 'Old Blazes' Message in smock and trousers tied at the knees with yokes, pulls a heavy turn-wrest plough, with its solid oak beam, at Jenkin's Town in c. 1890. Directing the plough is one of the Beal brothers.

THE WAR BILL IN TUN INN can trace its history back to 1690, when it was originally called The Two Tuns. Local legend claims its current name refers to a War of the Roses incident when marauding soldiers smashed open a barrel of beer (a tun) using a battle axe (a war bill), hence the current inn sign which shows a barrel with an axe embedded in it. Less interesting, but probably more accurate, is that the name is a deliberate pun on the village name. Upstairs can be found a smuggler's spy-hole.

THE OLD POOR-HOUSE, opposite the parish church of St Mary's, was purchased in 1825 by Warbleton's parish officers to provide for the poor and needy during the economic depression in the rural areas following the Napoleonic Wars. When Hailsham Union, with its poorhouse at Hellingly, took responsibility for the paupers in all the local parishes in 1834, Warbleton's workhouse held nineteen occupants. The lych-gate was erected at the entrance to the churchyard in 1909.

Vine's Cross

THE BREWER'S ARMS. When it was run by the Booth family, John Booth had a saddlery workshop erected in the front garden, behind the fencing. By the time of this 1930s postcard, the workshop had been demolished. The pub remains a tied house for Beard's Ales, the Lewes brewer, sixty years later.

BREAD DELIVERY CART outside A. Barrow's baker's and grocery shop, which also served until around 1908 as Vine's Cross's post office – it is now a private dwelling. St James' church, a corrugated iron chapel with a tin roof, was built alongside in 1911 on the site of the bakery storehouse. (c. 1905)

LOOKING SOUTH AT THE VINE'S CROSS JUNCTION, with John Bourner's smithy on the right. Two of the posters announce local celebrations for George V's coronation in 1911. To its immediate right stood the carpentry workshop of Frederick Pinniger who also acted as the local undertaker. (c. 1910)

REPLACING A TYRE at John Bourner's smithy with the Brewer's Arms behind, before its porches had been added. The wooden cart-wheel is placed on the metal tyring plate, with an anvil on the hub to hold it down. The red-hot iron tyre is then dropped over it and hammered firmly into position with the sledgehammer. Water is then poured on to the tyre, causing it to cool quickly and contract, thus gripping the cart-wheel tightly. (c. 1910)

A BEAUTIFUL PHOTOGRAPHIC STUDY of Charles Gates, with his distinctive bushy moustache, alongside his blazing forge in c. 1934. The smithy was demolished in 1958 for Vine's Cross Engineers to be built on its site.

THE NEXT SITE FOR THE VILLAGE POST OFFICE was at Harry Master's shop on the corner of Ballsocks Lane. He was also a local farmer and acted as an agent for 'keep sheep', sheep which would overwinter on another farmer's land. Along the lane can be seen the distinctive frontage of the Gospel Hall. By the 1970s its congregation had so dwindled that it was sold and converted into a private dwelling. (1912)

THE ELEMENTARY SCHOOL AT VINE'S CROSS, sometimes nicknamed the Clappers school, was erected in 1894 for ninety-four pupils. It was closed as a school in the 1960s and, for a number of years, was used as a store for the county's camping equipment. It has now been converted to a private dwelling. (c. 1930)

Horeham Road

HOREHAM ROAD POST OFFICE – the present site – in c.1925, with Molly Line (telegraph girl), Ernest Lemon (sub-postmaster), Arthur Lemon (son), Dorothy Smith (counter) and Mrs Arthur Lemon. In 1925 it was decided to change the village name as rail freight was sometimes misdirected to Horsham and parcel deliveries were delayed as carriers sought in vain for an actual road called Horeham Road. Villagers were invited to select a name and, at a public meeting on 12 November, the following votes were cast: Horam 98, Horamhurst 35, South Waldron 5, Great Waldron 4. Other suggestions (Horeham Cross, Horeham, Horehamly, Horamligh, Horehome, Mansfield, Horefield, Somerfield, Somerdale) received no votes at all. Although the village agreed to abide by this decision and adopted the name 'Horam' from this date, the telephone exchange perversely kept to the original name, with its new spelling 'Horam Road'.

W. DELVES was well stocked as the grocer, draper and general outfitter in 1902. It is easy to see why this was known locally as Delves' Corner. The first shop for W. Delves was opened at Maynards Green. A sign in the window advertises a furnished cottage to let.

DELVES' CORNER has become Creamery Corner by 1940, named after the Express Dairy Company's depot just around the corner in Vine's Cross Road. Its tankers were a common sight in those days. The car is parked outside the Horam Young Men's Club. Billiards and snooker were played downstairs while table tennis and social functions took place upstairs.

THE BUTCHER'S SHOP OF W. RUMARY AT DELVES' CORNER sold home-killed meat, dairy-fed pork and fresh sausages. The Rumary family owned considerable property in the area and, along with the Delves family who also owned the shop at Maynards Green, were well-respected entrepreneurs.

DELVES' CORNER at the turn of the century looks quite prosperous with W. Delves standing outside his shop, watching the pony and trap in front of A.G. Phillips, builder, and with W. Rumary, the butcher, to the right.

AT THE ENTRANCE TO MANOR ROAD, by the railway bridge, was the draper's shop and the office of O.H. Swann, the solicitor (also at Heathfield). The forge of Jim Funnell stood behind these buildings in Manor Road. The Oaks on the left was built in 1908 and is now a DIY and model shop. (1910)

THE SIGNWRITER MUST HAVE BEEN KEPT BUSY AT THE STATION with its frequent change of name: initially 'Horeham Road for Waldron' (1880), then 'Horeham Road and Waldron' (1890), 'Waldron and Horeham Road' (1900), 'Horeham Road' (1935), and finally 'Horam'. Note the milk churns on the platform. Originally farmers brought their milk to the station in churns and it was then transferred to the milk tank wagons. The working timetable for 1934 mentions a special milk train to Eastbourne at 8.20 p.m. (1915)

A GROCERY SHOP has stood on the High Street on the site of the current Spar shop since before the turn of the century. Here the proprietor and his wife, believed to be Mr and Mrs E. Funnell, pose at the doorway. (c. 1900)

Horeham Road, Sussex 7

HOREHAM ROAD POST OFFICE has again moved, this time into the High Street, just two doors away from its present site. Tolman & Co., auctioneer and estate agent, occupied the Bank Buildings. F.T. Turner, builder and undertaker, has since moved further along the High Street. (1916)

AT THE TURN OF THE CENTURY the horse and cart were the main users of the road. The first houses built in the High Street were the pair shown in the picture. Bank Buildings are not yet built and Horeham Manor is sited behind the trees on the right. (1910)

THE EASTBOURNE FOXHOUNDS, who hunted a wide area in 1905, have assembled outside R. Baker's tea house. The illustration looks down towards Station Approach. No buildings appear on the left of the High Street. (1907)

STATION APPROACH on leaving the 'Up' train to Tunbridge Wells and walking from the booking office, past the coal yard. Beyond the 'Dangerous Corner' warning sign are the established shops of Barrow Bros, Home & Colonial, Newnham Bros, drapers, outfitters & family grocer, and R. Baker's Tea Gardens. (1915)

STATION APPROACH is more populated by the 1930s. Whatleys Garage trades as Horeham Road Motor Works and sells Shell petrol from a single pump. E.J. Hoad has a bootshop where National Westminster Bank now operates. (1935)

STREAM FARM, at the bottom of Stillyans Hill, nestles below the railway line. The embankment allowed easier passage for the steam train in comparison with the steepness of the hill for road vehicles. The men who built the railway lived in a long wooden hut, just out of sight on the right of this picture, which was subsequently used as the scout hut.

STILLYANS HILL looks very treacherous on the downhill stretch towards Horeham Road. Stillyan's Oast has yet to be built and the railway embankment lacks vegetation and trees. Stillyan's Tower on the left cannot be seen. (1923)

TAKEN FROM THE RAILWAY LINE, this was the first view of Horeham Road seen by the rail traveller on the 'Down' line from Heathfield station. Stream Farm is in the bottom left corner with Bridge Cottages (built in 1904) behind. The houses painted in half-white are Streamside, Netherwood House, The Briars, Honeywell, The Firs, Oakfield, Brooklyn, Roselea and Homestead. The houses in Vines Cross Road can be seen beyond.

LEAVING DELVES' CORNER on the Heathfield Road, we see The Firs, Oakfield and Brooklyn. On the right are Bridge Cottages. The houses on the left-hand side of the road are officially on Maynards Green Road, while those on the right (out of picture) are classified as being on the High Street.

HOREHAM MANOR can just be seen through the trees and stood where the Merrydown Wine Company now operates. The manor (built in 1710 and burnt down in 1940) was a hotel and tea was provided at the Oast Tea Rooms. (1932)

THE WAR MEMORIAL has been moved from its original position in an enclosed field alongside the vicarage to the church in Horbeech Lane. The vicarage has since become a restaurant and more recently a used-car forecourt. The parsonage was originally opposite the church and is now called Oakroyd.

THE COUNCIL ESTATE was built in the early 1950s with its entrance opposite the church. Originally Tollwood Road was built before Beauford Road. 'Scotts' Pond was only recently filled in and became the green in front of Beauford Road when the estate was extended.

HOREHAM ROAD ARTILLERY COMPANY pictured at Stillyans (now St Mary's school), the residence of Major Young. Before the First World War regular training and drill were undertaken under the instruction of Sergeant Major Renham.

VINE'S CROSS ROAD looking towards Paynsbridge appears quite tranquil before the development of the Paynsbridge estate in the 1970s. Don Cockell who fought Rocky Marciano for the heavyweight boxing championship of the world lived at Diamonds Farm in Vine's Cross Road. (c. 1918)

GAMELANDS WESLEYAN CHURCH still stands at Coggers Cross although the attendance has since diminished. The heavy volume of traffic on the main A267 caused the church to move its original entrance into Swann Lane. (c. 1903)

A SPECIAL SIDING TO THE EXPRESS DAIRY COMPANY was laid to meet the 'Down' line at Horeham Road station in the late 1930s. Milk traffic was considerable at this time. The iron pedestrian bridge which spanned the road is not yet in evidence.

SHARPS CORNER was very quiet in 1920 and walking in the middle of the road was not a hazard. No footpaths had yet been laid, nor had the road surface yet been given its tarmac finish. Note the signpost does not point to Waldron; perhaps because Horeham Road was in the parish of Waldron.

THE SIGN ABOVE THE MILK CART shows A.J. Willmott as the licensee of the May Garland inn. Just past the bicycle hangs a sign above the door where Alfred Noakes operated the grocer's shop and post office. For over thirty years the inn was in the hands of the Lovely family.

HOREHAM ROAD POST OFFICE at Little London Road with Fernyhough's Library next door. The station booking office was the first place in Horeham where postage stamps could be bought, but thereafter the post office was at the May Garland, Manor Road, Paygate Cottages and then here. Read's Garage now occupies both these shops and the forecourt. (c. 1910)

A MOBILE HAY PRESS AT WORK, probably at Stillyans Farm. Considerable pressure could be exerted with such a long lever, ensuring that the block of hay which has been cut from the rick behind was compressed as firmly as possible. It could then be easily transported.

HORAM BOWLS CLUB, c. 1940. The Constance Scott Recreation Ground was given to the parish in 1938 and casual dress was the order of the day for village bowlers. Among those standing are Messrs Lambird, Message (Punnett's Town), Muddle, Wickens, Brooks, Turner, Smith, Monk and Col. Fermour. The bowler is Reg Turner.

CHARLIE MARLER originally set up his business in a coal shed at the rear of his house but then had the wooden workshop built near the old village hall in Horebeech Lane by the railway bridge. It was demolished in 1935 when he moved to a shop on the High Street next to the railway bridge.

SPORTS DAY AT MURRAY'S SCHOOL, a co-educational independent school for boarders and day pupils, on the Little London Road. The three single-storeyed classrooms adjoined the home of headmaster Walter Murray, the well-known naturalist, lecturer and writer. It closed in 1965. (c. 1940)

Maynards Green
and
Little London

THE CONGREGATION assembles on the rising ground outside the Gospel Hall on Whit Monday 1914. The Gospel Hall was moved to its present site in June 1905 as the old chapel was no longer large enough.

LOOKING NORTH ALONG THE MAIN ROAD before it was widened, with the Anglican chapel of ease on the left. It was built of brick in the Early English style in 1863 with a seating capacity of 100. Strangely, the 1875 Ordnance Survey map clearly marks the building as an infants' school. It has now been converted into a private dwelling. (Late 1930s)

THE ORIGINAL SIXTEENTH-CENTURY BUILDING of the Runt in Tun. By the early nineteenth century it served as a butcher's shop but then became an ale-house (an inn allowed to sell beer only). It is now divided into two cottages immediately alongside the current pub of that name. The distinctive wooden stairway and the chestnut tree to the left have only disappeared in recent years. (1908)

THE LANDLORD, TOM WHEATLY, AN EX-LONDON POLICEMAN, had Maynards Green builder and farmer John Curtis build the new Runt in Tun in 1910. Posing with their tools are Will Cornwall, George Hook, Solomon Cornwall, John Curtis (the builder's son who died later on the Somme), George Hendley, Charlie Pettit, John Curtis (with magnificent white whiskers), Herbert Baldwin and Tom Wheatley (the landlord).

THE NEW BUILDING OF THE RUNT IN TUN shortly after its completion. The ale licence was transferred from the old inn but it was not until the early 1920s when the locals organized a petition requesting a wine licence that stronger drinks could be consumed. Two bombs fell nearby in 1940; one blew the gas main near the entrance and caused a fire; the other destroyed a greenhouse at the old inn. (c. 1910)

LOOKING NORTH along what was then a narrow unmade road in 1910, past the original Gospel Hall, known locally as Delves' Chapel. The old chapel, with the sixteenth-century Stuckles Farm and Barn Cottage set behind it, has since been used for storage and even as an artist's studio. It lost its porch when the road was widened. Just past the hall was Greenfield's butcher's shop.

A POSED PHOTOGRAPH OF THE CONGREGATION outside the Gospel Hall, with a placard announcing, 'It is time to seek the Lord'. The strange vehicle is a wicker spinal carriage, like an elongated pram. Alongside it stands a Shirley Temple look-alike, in a short gingham dress with a big bow in her blonde hair – such a contrast to the staid appearance of the other children.

AN ITINERANT PREACHER, retired Police Inspector Elphick, with his gospel van at Maynard's Farm, with the farmer's children, Connie, Ron, Vera and Theo Delves. Local farmers would be responsible for supplying horses to collect the van from its previous venue and for housing the preacher during his one-week stay at the village, while he preached at the Gospel Hall. (c. 1930)

ITINERANT PREACHER, G. Coomber, has pitched his marquee in the field opposite the Gospel Hall before the houses were built. Left to right: Trayton Delves; A.E. Rumary; G. Coomber (preacher); William Delves; Walter Delves; Richard Rumary; Edwin Delves.

MAYNARDS GREEN SCHOOL was built in 1879 for 150 children, its catchment area including the children of Horeham Road. Initially the school had four classes but by 1881 this had been increased to six. (1905)

MEMBERS OF HEATHFIELD AND WALDRON'S FIRE BRIGADE pose on their original Ford fire-engine. The building on the right is Maynards Green School. (c.1926)

THE ORIGINAL BUILDING OF WILLIAM DELVES' GENERAL STORE, selling groceries, clothing and animal foodstuffs. Externally the shop has changed but little; the adjoining house, however, with its bricked-in central window, had a large new extension added across its whole frontage early in the twentieth century.

MR PARKES, who looked after the corn and meal trade at William Delves' shop, unloads sacks of flour at the bakehouse at the rear of the premises. The faggot stack stood alongside, as fuel for the oven. Note the 1s. 6d. deposit on the sack, and the date – 1924.

A HORSE-DRAWN HAY RAKE turns over the cut hay to allow it to dry evenly. Hay which is still damp when added to the rick is likely to generate heat as it decomposes and this is a frequent cause of haystack fires.

HORSE-DRAWN BINDER at work. The need for three horses suggests the machinery itself is heavy or perhaps the ground is uneven. Note the length of whip which is necessary to reach the lead horse.

BUILDING THE RICK. The farmhands use short pitchforks to unload the hay from the Sussex waisted wagon, a design of cart which allowed the high front wheels an increased amount of manoeuvrability. The haypoles, with the ladder balanced precariously against them, allowed for the hay to be piled much higher in the wagon.

AN ARMITAGE AND RUSTON 8NHP PORTABLE STEAM ENGINE powers a Marshall threshing machine on the farm. On hire from John Barnes of Bodle Street, it would have been hauled to this site by horses, hence the shaft at the front. Note the wooden wheels and the absence of a driver's footplate. I must admit to being impressed by the beautiful thatching of the hayricks. (c.1920)

AN ITINERANT MAT MENDER tries to repair the frayed edges of a footmat at Maynards Green. A seventeen-gallon milk churn stands on the bricks. (c. 1928)

TINKERS CARRY OUT BASIC REPAIR WORK on two chairs in the open air at Maynards Green. The man is rethreading the cane seat on one, while the woman repairs the upholstery on a balloon back chair.

THE OLD ROAD BY FRIARY WALK meandered in a more leisurely fashion in 1905. The chapel on the left is clearly visible, but, according to the 1875 Ordnance Survey map, this was originally the infants' school for the village. It is now a private dwelling.

TUBWELL LANE with Bath Cottages on the right looks almost unchanged today.

A GENERAL UTILITY WAGON in front of a corrugated tin farm building at Maynards Green. It is lightly laden so only a light harness is required. The netting over the wagon suggests it may be carrying livestock (lambs or perhaps a pig). (Late 1920s)

LOOKING SOUTH ALONG LITTLE LONDON ROAD towards Horeham Road (c. 1904) with the cottage Sunnyside on the left. Local tradition maintains that the hamlet acquired its name when Elizabeth I was passing through and quipped, 'Why, 'tis a veritable little London'.

THE VIEW ACROSS LITTLE LONDON'S TRIANGULAR GREEN shows a Union Jack fluttering in the distance in front of The Cottage. To the left is The Old Cannon House, now rebuilt after fire damage.

THE ROAD TO CROSS IN HAND, looking towards Piper's General Stores at Little London, before the building of the filling station alongside. On the right is the Strict Baptist Chapel, now being converted into a private dwelling. (c. 1920)

LITTLE LONDON POST OFFICE is now the office of Salvidge's Garage. The poster advertises 'Animated Pictures' (silent films) at the Recreation Hall, Heathfield, on 13 April 1914: *The Master Crook* with supporting film *Girl and the Outlaw*.

PIPER'S GENERAL STORES, formerly the post office, with a lovely enamel advert for Mansion Polish on the wall, in 1938. The poster advertises the films *Gangway* and *Oh, Mr Porter!* at the Plaza cinema at Heathfield. Unlike at modern tied garages, there were three different brands of petrol on offer at the pumps of the filling station: National Benzine, Shell and Essolene.

SECTION NINE

Waldron

LUCAS MEMORIAL HALL, here bedecked with celebratory flags and garlands, presumably for George V's 1911 coronation, was built in 1904 by Joseph Lucas of Foxhunt Manor, in memory of his wife, and was presented to the village in 1919. As a local benefactor he also gave the adjoining recreation ground, known locally as the Cattam, to the village.

THE STAR INN, a sixteenth-century building, still retains much of its quaint charm with massive oak beams and an inglenook fireplace with an ironback dated 1694. It even served as the village post office during the 1950s, having to close its counter during the actual licensing hours. The village square looks strangely empty without the war memorial cross. (c. 1900)

EBENEZER DAW'S village stores, with a bakehouse at the rear, stood facing the war memorial. It was converted into a private dwelling comparatively recently and has had its frontage so refaced that it is scarcely recognizable as 'Daw's'.

THE WAR MEMORIAL CROSS was unveiled in the village square on 25 July 1920. By the time the Second World War was over, the memorial had the names of seventy-five parishioners inscribed on it.

WAR MEMORIAL, WALDRON

THE VILLAGE BLACKSMITH, Mr Cheek, worked in the forge (the low building, now demolished, which adjoined his sixteenth-century cottage) until c. 1953. For several years, until 1947, he also ran the village post office from here.

A VIEW OF WALDRON from the church tower, showing on the left the rear of the village school, built to replace an earlier church school which had operated since 1714. Built to accommodate 150 children, it was adopted as a National School in 1876 and was finally closed in 1969. (c. 1910)

A VIEW ALONG WALDRON STREET showing the butcher's shop of Rogers & Son, now a general store and the only surviving shop in the village. The single-storey building to the left was for many years a shop selling sweets and cigarettes. (1913)

A TROOP OF LOCAL BOY SCOUTS form up outside Charlie Humphrey's shop, one of the many sites in the twentieth century for the village post office. Further along the road can be seen the distinctive window of the Lucas Memorial Hall. (c. 1910)

A MARSHAL 7HP STEAM TRACTION ENGINE drives a threshing machine at Cross Farm. The chaff falls to the ground underneath the machine; the grain is bagged up in the attached sacks; the hay is carried up the conveyor belt to the rick on the left. Behind can be seen the roof of the eleventh-century tithe barn with the distinctive chimneys of the farmhouse itself rising above it. (c. 1910)

HORSE-DRAWN TUMBLE-CART at Cross Farm, now St George's Vineyard. The small barn with its corrugated roof has now been converted into the farm shop. The cart is almost certainly the same one as in the illustration above, while Bob Stevenson, with the fork, (here accompanied by Jesse Kemp) also appears as a much younger man leading the ox team at Possingworth. (c. 1935)

BRAILSHAM COTTAGE on Back Lane, just to the south of Whitehouse Lane, was originally three cottages. The building further along is Haymakers Farm.

FOXHUNT GATE, looking along Foxhunt Road towards Foxhunt Green Farm, to the south of Waldron. The roundel of the oast-house can just be seen, adjoining the farmhouse itself which has the date 1678 carved on one of its main beams. (c. 1930)

CROSSWAYS is the name given to the junction of four lanes to the west of Waldron. The well-manicured yew trees in front of Crossways Cottage (originally three cottages but now converted into one) have been trimmed so low that they are now hidden behind the high hedges. (1910)

MAYPOLE DANCING on Waldron's recreation ground (with the village hall behind) to celebrate George V's silver jubilee in May 1935. Supervising the local children is headmistress Miss E.P.M. Morrison. Behind the cameraman stood the village workhouse, 'The Spike', now Grove Cottages.

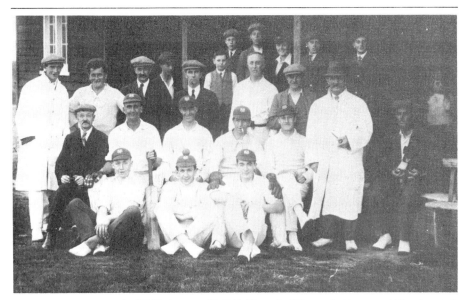

WALDRON CRICKET TEAM in 1923, the year Mr R.E. Hassell of Tanner's Manor paid for the pitch on the the recreation ground to be levelled and the pavilion built in memory of his brother, Colonel D. Bray Hassell, who died during the First World War. The team members were as follows – Standing, left to right: Mr Smith, Alec Hunniset, Jack Winter, Harold Gear, rector Stevenson, Eric Pettit, Bob Robins, Bert Westgate. Seated: Mr Edwards, Sam Oliver, Bert Smith, Bert Edwards, Arthur Westgate. Ground: Jim Hamper, Jack Hollands, Gilbert Hook. Children at the rear include Francis Daw, Jack Burgess and Robert Daw.

WALDRON FOOTBALL TEAM poses in front of the village hall. I presume their eleventh player is taking the photograph. (1907)

OLD POSSINGWORTH.

THE ESTATE WORKERS OF THE OLD MANOR HOUSE of Possingworth, built in 1657 for Thomas Offley. During the Second World War it was occupied by Canadian troops and some of the D-Day invasion plans are believed to have been drawn up here. (1912)

Cross in Hand

THE GENERAL STORES OF W.S. BURT seems to have sold almost anything. The advert mentions groceries, drapery, glass and chinaware, while outside trugs, wicker baskets and hoops are on display. (1912)

CROSS IN HAND USED TO BOAST TWO WINDMILLS. The old post-mill, with its roundhouse, had stood for centuries, was hand-winded, and was still working until 1903, when one of her stocks broke and it was found too expensive to repair her. The larger post-mill was only brought from Mount Ephraim, Framfield, in 1855 by miller William Kenward, but local landowner, Squire Huth, objected to its position and it was moved 400 yd south-west to its present site in 1868. From 1888 the millers were the Newnham and Ashdown families. The New Mill ceased operating after a stock broke in 1969. It was the last working mill in Sussex. (c. 1890)

NEWNHAM AND ASHDOWN'S first motorized delivery vehicle was this 1 ton Model T Ford lorry, with solid tyres on the back, which they bought in 1924.

THEIR SECOND DELIVERY VEHICLE was this 1931 Bedford lorry, laden with sacks of grain. Standing in the entrance to the roundhouse of the New Mill is Jack Ashdown. (1931)

A GARDENING LESSON for the boys of Cross in Hand school in 1924. Pupils were allocated their own plots of land to look after, but were also expected to work on Mr A.W. Marsh the headmaster's garden, behind the shed on the right.

THE ROAD FROM CROSS IN HAND TO LEWES was originally a turnpike road, i.e. a road where a toll was payable. The toll keeper's cottage, on the right of the photograph, used to control the junction with a gate, but, when tolls were abolished in 1841, other uses had to be found for such properties.

CROSS IN HAND HOTEL has been one of the hubs of village life over the centuries – in fact some of the building's features can be dated to c. 1600. From 1883 to 1970 the hotel was run by various members of the Seamer family. The delivery bicycle belongs to Thurston's, the local butcher. The car looks like a rather fancy French model.

BY THE TURN OF THE TWENTIETH CENTURY Horace Thorpe, with steel-rimmed spectacles, had transformed the toll keeper's cottage into a bicycle repair shop and was later to turn his mechanical talents to repairing motor vehicles, when he opened his garage at the top of Pages Hill. His assistant, Eric Eastwood, stands in the doorway. The 'Open & Closed Cars' for hire are presumably saloons and tourers.

PITHER'S GARAGE used to stand alongside the inn on the opposite side of the road from the site of the current petrol station. Here a Bedford tanker stands on the forecourt to refill the underground petrol tanks. (c. 1950)

THE BAKERY OF JAMES HERRING and his wife Maggy originally stood on the corner, directly opposite the general stores, with its shop entrance on the main Mayfield Road. Although the bakery has long been demolished, marks of the ridge of the roof are still clearly to be seen on the side wall of the Corner House. They later moved their premises to where Bell's now operate their bakery. (c. 1898)

CROSS IN HAND POST OFFICE in 1910. At this time the sub-postmistress was Mrs Amelia Jane Saunders. Although the shop window is still in position, there is currently no shop on this site.

ALMA VILLA stands behind the trees on the left, which include a very tall monkey puzzle tree, so fashionable in the Victorian era. Further along on the left several generations of the Jarvis family have run their business as builders and undertakers. (c. 1910)

THE BELLE VUE INN, now the private dwelling Chillington, served as a local hostelry – and later as a post house, where the mail coach would stop overnight and change horses, etc. – from 1790 until early in the twentieth century. Behind the landlord and the monkey puzzle tree can be seen the inn's stables.

CROSS IN HAND HORSE SHOW was held each August in what are now the Hardy Roberts Playing Fields. As well as all the events traditionally associated with horse shows, travelling fairs would set up their roundabouts, stalls and sideshows. On the following day the local children were allowed to attend free of charge. The crowd might also be entertained by local activities – see cover photograph!

THE FIRGROVE ROAD JUNCTION has changed remarkably little since this 1910 photograph. The Methodist congregation had to meet at Glovers chapel, a converted barn at Firgrove farmhouse, before the church was built in 1896. Beaconsfield Terrace leads downhill to the left. During the Second World War, No. 4 had a narrow escape from a German bomb which blew up the water and gas mains outside.

THE FIR GROVE which gave its name to Firgrove Road used to stand along the road at the junction with Brown's Lane (on the right). The bungalow has long been demolished, leaving no trace in the field, but the wall on the left is still there, in front of The Old Farm.

LOOKING NORTH AT ROSER'S CROSS, on the road from Crossways, in 1910. To the left of this junction lies Warren Road, while Firgrove Road leads off to Cross in Hand. Several properties were soon to be built in the triangle of land between the finger-post and the footpath.

THE CROWDS – and their carriages – attend a society wedding at St Bartholomew's church (built in woodland in 1863) in 1907. A canopy has been set up leading from the road down to the church itself. The house in the background, now Church Cottage, served as Cross in Hand's National School from 1876 to 1898.

CROSS IN HAND SCHOOL was built at Mount Pleasant in 1899 to replace the earlier national school. A new infant school was built at Sheepsetting Lane in 1969, but the school was not finally closed until 1985 when the junior pupils were transferred to the new building. (1907)

PUPILS OF CROSS IN HAND SCHOOL can be seen on the right on their playing field to the west of Snatchells Farm where they played organized games of cricket, rounders, stoolball, etc. (c. 1910)

LOOKING WEST ALONG THE MAIN ROAD from Heathfield to Cross in Hand. The cart track entrance on the left marks Pages Hill.

A WINTER'S SCENE along Little London Road, with New Pond Hill on the right. Horace Thorpe would later build his garage behind the hedge on the left in the land between Pages Hill and Sheepsetting Lane. The hoarding advertises Charlie Ryder's garage on the High Street. The Victorian postbox on the right has recently been moved to a new position down Pages Hill.

HORACE THORPE'S GARAGE, now Pine Garage, on Little London Road began life as a converted barn. The petrol pump had to be hand cranked. The crank handle itself had to be taken indoors for security after each filling and the hinged covers were locked each evening.

NEW POND HILL used to have its own grocery shop, run by Mrs Collins, in the house known as Danns. When her daughter, Lottie Elliott, transferred the business to the shop at the south end of Back Lane in c. 1940, she took her shop's display window with her! The magnificent bay tree on the left survived until only a few years ago. (1903)

PEACE DAY CELEBRATIONS are believed to have been held at Lanrick, on Back Lane, the home of Major and Mrs Twynam, who had suffered the loss of their only son during the war. They were to dedicate the war shrine at St Bartholomew's to his memory. Major Twynam was to become the first commandant of the Waldron branch of the British Legion in 1921.

POSSINGWORTH was built as an elaborate neo-Gothic mansion for Louis Huth in 1866 at a cost of £60,000. It became a grand hotel in the 1930s; was bought in the 1950s as a seminary for Augustinian priests; and since 1964 has been a religious nursing home run by an order of nuns.

A TEAM OF YOKED OXEN draws a Sussex waisted wagon laden with timber, with the distinctive fencing of Possingworth Park behind. Bob Stevenson stands at the cart, with Jack Evenden holding the goad, a tipped stick used for prodding the oxen into activity since a whip was often ignored by the thick-skinned creatures. Note the double-width wheel rims. (1903)

A FINE STUDY OF THE GAMEKEEPERS – and their splendid mutton chop whiskers – employed on the Possingworth estate. Life was obviously good for them since they have all reached respectable old age, with a combined working life of an impressive 114 years. I wonder how often we would come across such job loyalty today.

WARREN CORNER, the westerly limit of Cross in Hand. The main road on the right follows the route of the old turnpike road to Lewes. Behind the tree can just be seen The Old House, a stone dwelling erected in 1836. (1916)

MEMBERS OF CROSS IN HAND'S COURT NO. 7697 of the Ancient Order of Foresters pose with their sashes, medals and the magnificent banner.

WOODCOTE, opposite Scocus Farm, was part of the Isenhurst estate until c. 1910, when it had the extension on the left added. During the First World War it served as a convalescent hospital for wounded servicemen. At this time a wooden shed was added at the rear to serve as an office and medical store. The nurses lived at The Dell, behind the cottage to the left of Woodcote. (c. 1916)

Five Ashes

The Village, Five Ashes.

THE VILLAGE GREEN, before the erection of the war memorial or the planting of the five ashes. Amos Tobitt poses on the forecourt of his general store which also served as the village post office, while William Petitt poses in the doorway of the Five Ashes Inn, behind the row of five pollarded lime trees which were planted in 1892 to commemorate his five daughters. (They were only chopped down in 1976.) (1908)

CROUST FARM, ON SUMMER HILL, to the south of Five Ashes, stands beside the old turnpike road to Hadlow Down at The Crossways, the now busy junction of the A272 and A267. The T-junction looks so different today, having lost its triangle of greenery and its finger post. (1910)

THE VILLAGE GREEN, with one of the five ashes alongside the stone war memorial (blown down in the great storm of October 1987). The five ashes were provided by Mr Nicholson of Skipper's Hill Manor and were planted in 1912 by Alfred Berwick, at various times landlord of the inn and shopkeeper. The village had a quoits team which played on a quoits bed opposite the inn, near the Model T Ford lorry, until the 1930s. (c. 1922)

FIVE ASHES NATIONAL SCHOOL was built on land alongside the turnpike road from Mayfield to Hadlow Down in 1872 as a mixed elementary and primary school for sixty pupils but had to be further extended in 1904 to accommodate 125 pupils. It was not until 1932 that mains water was supplied and 1938 when electric lighting was installed. (1911)

THE VILLAGE STORES. The white weather-boarded cottage with the corrugated roof was Boaz Eastwood's bakery (now a private dwelling, Primrose Cottage). In 1902 he had the house built, with the adjoining single-storey general store (now demolished). Directly opposite this scene a filling station has since been built. (c. 1920)

RISINGHOLME, the Eastwood family home, had two workshops behind it. Jim Eastwood, local builder and undertaker, stands in the doorway of his carpentry and undertaker's workshop. He stored building equipment in the shed on the left. Leaning on the builder's cart is Noah Eastwood, while his brother Frederick wears the straw boater. Two bungalows now occupy this site while the house has changed its name to Shrubs Hill. (c. 1890)

THE SMITHY AND WHEELWRIGHT'S WORKSHOP of William Reeves which stood at Butcher's Cross, to the north of Five Ashes, behind Toll Cottage, the converted toll-house for the old turnpike road. From 1921 it was worked by David and Percy Reeves. The smithy has been demolished and a bungalow built on its footings. (1910)

SECTION TWELVE
Hadlow Down

THE NEW INN was built on the site of an earlier New Inn which burnt down in mysterious circumstances – possibly arson – in the mid-1880s. The architect was believed to be Samuel Denman of Brighton whose expertise had been in designing churches, hence the inn's rather fanciful Victorian façade. A second plausible explanation for this feature was that the inn was intended to be the Railway Inn for a line which was never built. (1904)

LOOKING EAST ALONG SOUTH BEACON ROAD, the main road, with the Wilderness Lane junction on the right. The house in the distance served as the village police house. Further along on the right was South Beacon, which, together with the house across the road, was run as a private asylum by Dr Philip Harmer. (1916)

BEHIND THE MAGNIFICENT OAK TREE can be seen the Methodist chapel which now lies completely derelict, having suffered considerable structural damage in the great storm of 1987. The next house along is Preston Cottage, built in 1892 with an adjoining shop and bakehouse, for Alfred Smith. Here he sold bread, groceries, chicken feed and even coal.

LOOKING TOWARDS THE NEW INN with Percy Ireland's grocer's shop on the right. It also served as Hadlow Down's post office and telephone exchange. (c. 1902)

THE GENERAL SUPPLY STORE of Alfred 'Daddy' Barnes in 1915. Hardware was sold in the extension on the right. The building continued to serve as the village store until the 1960s when it became a café.

HADLOW DOWN'S ELEMENTARY SCHOOL was built on land given to the village by the Earl and Countess De La Warr in 1835 specifically for the building of a parish church, vicarage and village school. It could accommodate 170 pupils who originally had to pay one penny each for a week's tuition. Apart from the loss of the two chimneys there appears to be little external change. (1906)

LOOKING EAST towards the centre of the village, with School Lane on the left and the Wilderness Lane junction on the right. The house, Four Ways, has now been converted into a residential home for the elderly, Marlowe House.

A MEET OF THE SOUTHDOWN HOUNDS at Hadlow Grange, the home of Charles Lang Huggins JP, c. 1914. In 1913 he paid the entire cost of rebuilding the new parish church on the foundations of the demolished 1836 church. Although both the Southdown and Eridge Hunts would meet regularly at The Grange, the main road formed the dividing line between their hunting territories: Southdown to the south and Eridge to the north.

PARTICULARLY CONFUSING TO ALL DELIVERYMEN is the fact that both of the lanes at this junction claim to be called Wilderness Lane. Correctly the lane on the right of Woodgate, built c. 1810, should claim the name since it runs alongside Wilderness Wood.

A ROYAL VISIT to Hadlow Down when Princess Marie Louise arrived to open the Red Triangle Hut on 8 June 1921. The hut was presented by the YMCA (hence the red triangle, their badge), who had one of their wooden huts at Summerdown army camp (near Eastbourne) dismantled to be collected and re-erected by local labour. Behind the car can be seen Alfred Barnes' general store.

LOCAL GIRL GUIDES form a guard of honour for Princess Marie Louise along Hut Lane as she descends to the hut. Eventually it was presented to the parish to serve as the parish hall and has now been rebuilt in brick.

Blackboys

GEORGE BERRY'S BLACKBOYS INN can trace its history back to its building as a farmhouse in 1389. It was converted into an ale-house to service the needs of workers at the local iron foundries and then served as a coaching inn on the routes from London, via Uckfield, to the Sussex coast. The inn is reputed to be haunted by the ghost of Anne Starr who died in childbirth in an upstairs bedroom. (1914)

HENRY EADE'S CROWN INN, with carts parked up on the forecourt, stands on the Framfield Junction with Albert Burgess's grocery store and post office opposite.

HENRY HEMSLEY'S GUN INN has reverted to a farmhouse and, in more recent years, has also been developed into a squash club. The monkey puzzle tree has long since disappeared. (1908)

BLACKBOYS POST-MILL was erected to the west of the village in 1867–8, having been moved by teams of horses from its original site at Glynde, where it had stood since 1807. It was operated until c. 1935 by George and John Paris, who also ran the bakery opposite, but was eventually demolished in 1945, although some of its brick foundations can still be seen. (c. 1910)

BLACKBOYS SCHOOL was built in 1875 as a mixed elementary school and the school house was added in 1887 to commemorate Queen Victoria's Jubilee. By 1899 the number of pupils had increased so the building had to be extended to accommodate 147 children. The school has since been completely rebuilt. The master at the time of this photograph was Alfred Marsh, later to move to Cross in Hand School.

BLACKBOYS GENERAL STORES, run by Mrs Sarah Ann Baldwin, used to stand on the Framfield Road, on the junction with School Lane. The wooden shed on the left served as the workshop for one of three bootmakers in the village. The weather-boarded building has since been demolished. (c. 1919)

UPTON'S MILL was still a working watermill, operated by George Heaver, a local farmer and hop grower, when this photograph was taken. It stands one mile north-west of Blackboys but has long lost its waterwheel and been tastefully converted into a private dwelling, now called Heaver's Mill. (1905)

LOOKING NORTH ALONG THE LANE towards the watermill (distant left). The mill owner's cottage has retained the name Upton's Mill. (1905)

ACKNOWLEDGEMENTS

Grateful thanks are due to all of the following for the loan of photographic material and generous help with information:

B. & E. Barrow • A. Burgess • P. Burgess
P. Cole • N. Cook • R. Daw • R. & J. Delves
B. Delves • Mrs Farley • P.J. Love
C. & G. Marler • A. Perodeau
D. & M. Saunders • A.E. Stevenson • G. Wettle
J. Giles • J. Fuller • E. Bean • D. Godley
Mrs Funnell • Horsebridge Antiques • D. Neve
J. & M. Ashdown • R. & H. Whiteman
Mrs J. Smart • Mrs P. Simmonds
J. & J. Russell • M. Eldridge
Mrs A.E. Preece • R.G. & G.I. Eastwood
H. & S. Wylam • Heathfield WI • Five Ashes WI
Caffyns Archive • Lt. Col. P.E. Barton
N. McNally • F.S. Pope • Mrs W. Message
C.J. Newnham • Miss A. Gibbs •E. Pope
Mrs I. Tompsett • J. Bartholomew
Mrs H. Dann • R. Thorpe • A. Randall
and many others, too numerous to mention.